North Mary, My Service Mini Horse

North Mary, Mi Caballo Mini de Servicio

Written and Illustrated by William
Escrito e ilustrado por William

For information regarding discounts for bulk purchases or promotional applications of this book,
contact rob@writeawaybooks.com.

WRITE AWAY BOOKS
Taking Authors From Idea to Manuscript to Marketplace™

Published by Write Away Books
PO Box 1681, Carlsbad, CA 92018
www.writeawaybooks.com

Written and Illustrated by William
email: talktoauthorwilliam@gmail.com

Book design by Beth Hutchins Design
Lakeside, CA

ISBN 978-1-969838-05-7

First Edition

For North Mary,
Mom, Dad and Dana.

Para North Mary,
Mamá, Papá y Dana.

This is **North Mary**.
She is my service mini horse.
She is a mini horse, not a pony, and not a big dog.
She is light brown with a white mane and tail.

She feels soft and warm when I touch her.
She smells earthy, like dirt and grass at her trainer's ranch.

Esta es **North Mary**.
Es mi caballo mini de servicio.
Es un caballo mini, no es un pony y no es un perro grande.
Es color café claro con cabello y cola blancos.

Se siente suave y calientita cuando la toco.
Huele como la tierra y el pasto en el rancho de su entrenadora.

She is 30 inches tall.
I am 50 inches tall.

She is the perfect height for me.

Ella mide 30 pulgadas.
Yo mido 50 pulgadas.

Es la altura perfecta para mí.

First, I met a dark horse named **Frida**.

Frida was not right for me.
She was too fast.
Too energetic.
Not calm enough.

A service animal must match their person, and follow their lead.

Primero, conocí a un caballo oscuro de nombre **Frida**.

Frida no era la indicada para mí.
Era muy inquieta.
Tenía mucha energía.
No era muy tranquila.

Un animal de servicio debe conectar con su persona y seguir sus indicaciones.

Then I met **North Mary**.

She stood still.
She looked at me.
She neighed softly.

I knew she was different.
She was the perfect match for me.

Luego conocí a **North Mary**.

Se quedó quieta.
Me miró.
Relinchó suavemente.

Supe que era diferente.
Era perfecta para mí.

The day I brought **North Mary** home, she rode in the trainer's trailer.

I showed her her new home.

"Welcome home, **North Mary**," I said. "I'm happy that you are here."

That was one of the happiest days of my life.

El día que traje a **North Mary** a mi casa, viajó en el tráiler de su entrenadora.

Le enseñé su nuevo hogar.

"Bienvenida a casa, **North Mary**," le dije. "Estoy feliz de que estés aquí."

Fue uno de los días más felices de mi vida.

Life with **North Mary** is very special.

In the morning, I clean her stall. I give her food and make sure she has plenty of water.

She eats hay and grain. She likes lettuce leaves, carrots, bananas, apples and pears. She does not like celery or oranges.

Then she walks me to school. She knows the way.

La vida con **North Mary** es muy especial.

En la mañana, limpio su establo. Le doy comida y me aseguro de que tenga suficiente agua.

Come pasto y granos. Le gustan las hojas de lechuga, las zanahorias, los plátanos, las manzanas y las peras. No le gustan el apio ni las naranjas.

Luego me lleva a la escuela. Ella sabe el camino.

In the afternoon, **North Mary** helps me keep calm while:
I do homework.
I swim.
I do Taekwondo.
I ride big horses.
I play the piano.
I work on fun projects.
I play with my trains.
I practice riding my bike.
I play at the park.
I write books.

Then, **North Mary** takes me for a long walk. We walk at least twice a day.

At night I clean her stall again. Once more, I give her food and make sure she has plenty of water.

En la tarde, **North Mary** me ayuda a mantener la calma mientras:
Hago mi tarea.
Nado.
Practico Taekwondo.
Monto caballos grandes.
Toco el piano.
Trabajo en proyectos divertidos.
Juego con mis trenes.
Practico andar en bicicleta.
Juego en el parque.
Escribo libros.

Después, **North Mary** me lleva a dar una caminata larga. Caminamos por lo menos dos veces al día.

En la noche, limpio su establo de nuevo. Una vez más, le doy comida y me aseguro de que tenga agua.

North Mary is my service mini horse.

She helps me keep my balance. She helps me deal with big feelings. She helps me when I don't want to wait.

She keeps me safe. She makes sure I do not run away from my parents into unsafe places. She does not let me cross the street without an adult.

She calms me when I hug her. She makes me happy.

North Mary es mi caballo mini de servicio.

Me ayuda a mantener mi balance. Me ayuda con mis emociones grandes. Me ayuda cuando no quiero esperar.

Me mantiene seguro. Se asegura de que no corra lejos de mis papás hacia lugares peligrosos. No me deja cruzar la calle sin un adulto.

Me calma cuando la abrazo. Me hace feliz.

LIBRARY

Since I have her,
I show her love.
I give her hugs.
I write her notes.
I clean her stall.

I feed her.
I give her water.
I brush her hair.

She has helped me grow.

Desde que ella está conmigo,
yo le demuestro amor.
Le doy abrazos.
Le escribo notas.
Limpio su establo.

La alimento.
Le doy agua.
Cepillo su cabello.

Ella me ha ayudado a crecer.

When **North Mary** sees her **pink halter**, she knows it is time to work.

She does not need a vest to be a service horse. She is still a service horse even without it.

She knows spoken commands like:
Walk.
Head Up.
Working.
Whoa.
Trot.

She also understands quiet signals.

Her working face is calm.
Her breathing is soft.
She walks by my side.
Her lead rope feels secure in my hand.

Cuando **North Mary** ve su **cuerda rosa**, sabe que es hora de trabajar.

No necesita un chaleco para ser un caballo de servicio. Sigue siendo un caballo de servicio aunque no lo use.

Conoce órdenes como:
Camina.
Cabeza arriba.
Trabaja.
Alto.
Trota.

También entiende señales silenciosas.

Su cara de trabajo es tranquila.
Respira suave.
Camina a mi lado.
Su cuerda se siente segura en mi mano.

North Mary does not always wear her **pink halter**.

She knows she is working when she wears her halter and lead rope.

At home, she can have her halter off and take a break from working.

She can sleep.
She can eat.
She can go potty.
She can run.
She can play.
She can neigh.
She can stick out her tongue.
She can relax and be silly.

North Mary no siempre usa su **cuerda rosa**.

Sabe que está trabajando cuando usa su cuerda.

En casa, puede quitarse su cuerda y descansar.

Puede dormir.
Puede comer.
Puede ir al baño.
Puede correr.
Puede jugar.
Puede relinchar.
Puede sacar la lengua.
Puede relajarse y ser divertida.

Z
Z
Z
Z

When I have big feelings, **North Mary** reminds me to stay calm.

If you asked her, she would say I am her favorite.

When I brought her home, I told her I was happy she was here with me.

If someone says mini horses can't be service animals, I say:

"They can be. Look it up and read my book."

Cuando tengo emociones grandes, **North Mary** me recuerda mantener la calma.

Si le preguntaras, ella diría que yo soy su favorito.

Cuando la traje a casa, le dije que estaba feliz de que estuviera conmigo.

Si alguien dice que los caballos mini no pueden ser animales de servicio, yo digo:

"Sí pueden. Búscalo y lee mi libro."

Before **North Mary**, the store was hard for me.

I didn't want to wait.
I fidgeted.
I tripped.
I lost my balance.
I wanted to leave.

One day I brought **North Mary** to the store and someone said, "That's not a real service animal."

I felt sad.
I felt mad.
My body felt tight.
But **North Mary** helped me stay calm.

"She is my service horse," I said.

Antes de **North Mary**, la tienda era difícil para mí.

No quería esperar.
Me movía mucho.
Me tropezaba.
Perdía mi balance.
Quería irme.

Un día lleve a **North Mary** a la tienda y alguien dijo, "Ese no es un animal de servicio real."

Me sentí triste.
Me sentí enojado.
Mi cuerpo se sintió tenso.
Pero **North Mary** me ayudó a mantener la calma.

"Ella es mi caballo de servicio," dije.

SOUP
$9.99
$15.94
$9.99

Stores have a rule:
No animals.

But the law has a rule:
Yes to service animals.

The law is stronger.
This is a federal law.

Mini horses CAN be service animals. Only dogs and mini horses can be service animals.

Some stores have signs that show only dogs as service animals. That can be confusing.

Las tiendas tienen una regla:
No animales.

Pero la ley tiene otra regla:
Sí a los animales de servicio.

La ley es más fuerte.
Es una ley federal.

Los caballos mini SÍ pueden ser animales de servicio. Solo los perros y los caballos mini pueden ser animales de servicio.

Algunas tiendas muestran letreros con dibujos de perros de servicio solamente. Eso puede causar confusión.

Service animals only please

Animales de servicio solamente por favor

If a store breaks the law, they are wrong.

When someone does not know the law, you explain it. You show them this book. You tell them to look it up.

When **North Mary** is working:
- she cannot be petted.
- she cannot be distracted.
- she must be treated with respect.

That is fair.

Si una tienda no sigue la ley, está en un error.

Cuando alguien no conoce la ley, se la explicas. Le enseñas este libro. Le dices que lo busque.

Cuando **North Mary** está trabajando:
- no se le puede tocar.
- no se le puede distraer.
- debe ser tratada con respeto.

Eso es justo.

STORE

Fair means following the law.

If a store says "No animals" but the law says "Yes" to service animals, the law wins.

That makes it fair.

It also means respecting **North Mary's** space and my space.

Justo significa seguir la ley.

Si una tienda dice "No animales" pero la ley dice "Sí" a los animales de servicio," la ley gana.

Eso lo hace justo.

También significa respetar el espacio de **North Mary** y mi espacio.

I am a hero because I wrote this book to help people who need a service animal, but cannot have a dog.

North Mary is a hero because she is trained, calm and keeps me safe.

We are both heroes.

Yo soy un héroe porque escribí este libro para ayudar a personas que necesitan un animal de servicio, pero no pueden tener un perro.

North Mary es una heroína porque está entrenada, es tranquila y me mantiene seguro.

Los dos somos héroes.

North Mary is small.

But her job is big.

People should respect her.

We are a team.

North Mary es pequeña.

Pero su trabajo es grande.

Las personas deben respetarla.

Somos un equipo.

Under federal law (ADA), miniature horses can be service animals.

A mini horse service animal needs:

- A safe place to live (such as a barn)
- Space to move and exercise
- A horse trailer for safe travel
- Healthy food and fresh water
- Grooming and regular vet care
- Proper training for one specific person

Service mini horses are working animals; not pets. They require responsibility, space, and commitment.

For more information about service animals, visit **ADA.gov**.

Según la ley federal (ADA), los caballos miniatura pueden ser animales de servicio.

Un caballo miniatura de servicio necesita:

- Un lugar seguro para vivir (como un establo)
- Espacio para moverse y ejercitarse
- Un tráiler de caballos para viajar con seguridad
- Comida saludable y agua fresca
- Cuidado veterinario, mantenimiento y limpieza regular
- Entrenamiento para una persona específica

Los caballos miniatura de servicio son animales de trabajo; no mascotas. Requieren responsabilidad, espacio, y compromiso.

Para más información sobre animales de servicio, visite **ADA.gov**

About the Author

William is an author and junior advocate. He lives with his family and his service mini horse, **North Mary**.

He wrote this book to teach others that mini horses can be service animals under the law.

Sobre el Autor

William es un autor y defensor junior. Vive con su familia y su caballo mini de servicio, **North Mary**.

Escribió este libro para enseñar a otros que los caballos mini pueden ser animales de servicio según la ley.

www.ingramcontent.com/pod-product-compliance
Ingram Content Group UK Ltd.
Pitfield, Milton Keynes, MK11 3LW, UK
UKRC032309290726
14090UKWH00004B/405

9781969838057

9 781969 838057